HISTORY THROUGH
NewspApErs

The
Home Front in
WORLD
WAR II

Stewart Ross

HODDER
Wayland

an imprint of Hodder Children's Books

Produced for Hodder Wayland by
Discovery Books Ltd
Unit 3, 37 Watling Street, Leintwardine, Shropshire SY7 0LW

First published in 2002 by Hodder Wayland, an imprint of Hodder Children's Books

British Library Cataloguing in Publication Data
Ross, Stewart
The home front in World War Two. – (History through
newspapers)
1.World War, 1939-1945 – Social aspects – Great Britain –
Sources – Juvenile literature 2.World War, 1939-1945 –
Social aspects – Great Britain – Press coverage – Juvenile
literature 3.Great Britain – Social conditions – 20th
century – Sources – Juvenile literature 4.Great Britain –
Social conditions – 20th century – Press coverage –
Juvenile literature
I.Title
941'.084

ISBN 0750241845

Printed and bound in Italy by G. Canale & C.Sp.A, Turin

Designer: Ian Winton
Cover design: Claire Bond
Series editors: Jane Tyler and Kathryn Walker
Picture research: Rachel Tisdale

Learn.co.uk is a trade mark of Guardian Education Interactive Limited and is used under license

Hodder Children's Books would like to thank the following for the loan of their material:
Corbis: page 26/27; **Hulton Getty:** Cover, page 4/5, 6/7, 8/9, 12/13, 14/15, 16/17, 18/19, 23, 24/25; **Peter Newark's Picture Library:** 10/11; **Discovery Picture Library:** 20/21; **Mary Evans Picture Library:** 28/29.

Hodder Children's Books would like to thank the following for permission to reproduce newspaper articles: **by kind permission of Atlantic Syndication for Associated Newspapers:** page 6; ©**The Daily Mirror:** page 10, 28; © **Express Newspapers:** page 8; © **Learnthings Limited and Guardian Newspapers Limited:** page 14, 16, 20, 22, 26, ©**Telegraph Group Limited 1940:** page 18, 24.

Hodder Children's Books
A division of Hodder Headline Limited
338 Euston Road
London NW1 3BH

CONTENTS

NO ESCAPE!

On 1 September 1939 **Nazi** Germany invaded Poland. Britain and France demanded the German forces be withdrawn. Their demand was ignored and two days later Britain and France declared war on Germany.

The Home Front

By the end of 1941 the European conflict was one of several wars raging around the world. Together these are known as World War II. The only truly global war, it was the most widespread and costly in human history.

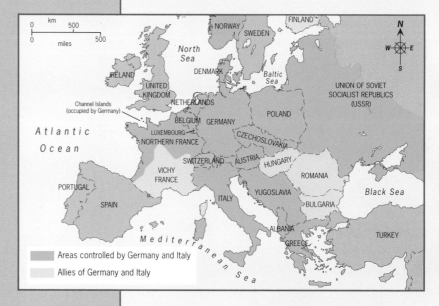

(*Above*) **The areas of Europe controlled by the fascist powers, Germany and Italy, at Christmas 1941.**

(*Left*) **The Blitzed cities – areas of Britain hardest hit by enemy bombing 1940-41.**

It was also a **'total' war** in which the warring states geared all their national resources – industrial, personnel, financial, agricultural and military – towards victory.

Traditionally, armies and navies fought at the battle **front**; civilians – those not in the **armed forces** – were only occasionally involved. With modern total war there was no escape. Everyone was involved, military personnel on the battle front and civilians on the 'home front'.

The home front affected British civilians in three ways. First, bombing put them in the firing line. In 1940 there was a very real threat of invasion, too. Second, many peacetime freedoms were removed. As part of the war effort the government took control of people's work, and even the food they ate and the clothes they wore. Finally, total war brought much hardship on the home front, including the rationing of everyday necessities.

There was little panic when war was declared in 1939. However, like the man smoking a cigarette in this picture, many people were quietly anxious.

Censorship

During the 1930s the BBC had run the world's first, small-scale television service. It was stopped in 1939. To find out what was going on – and during the war news was a top priority – Britons relied on newspapers and BBC radio. There was no independent radio and the only alternative to the BBC was enemy **propaganda** broadcasting.

Two Emergency Powers **Acts** (1939 and 1940) gave the government full powers of **censorship**: controlling what appeared in the print and broadcast **media**. The government preferred not to use these powers, however. Instead, the media was largely self-censoring – journalists tried not to print what the government would disapprove of. This raised problems. Newspaper editors had to decide whether criticizing the government's handling of, say, rationing would bring about improvement or undermine the country's leadership.

Issues like these need to be borne in mind when reading the extracts that follow. They were written to inform, but also to help in the struggle for victory. Consequently, they may not give a full or accurate picture of events. Their language is sometimes loaded, too – deliberately chosen to persuade the reader to a certain point of view. Note in particular the difference in the way the British and the enemy are described. (There is a good example on page 26.)

THE CALL UP

In May 1939, even before war broke out, the government began registering all men between the ages of eighteen and twenty-seven for war work. The great majority were destined for the armed services, particularly the army. This process, obliging people to join the forces, is known as '**conscription**', or 'call up'. Britain had first used it during World War I.

Conscription

After the outbreak of war all men found to be medically fit for service aged between eighteen and forty-one were liable for conscription, with two groups of exceptions. One was men in 'reserve occupations' – jobs that were of national importance, such as that of a doctor. The other was 'conscientious objectors' – those whose beliefs (usually religious) would not let them fight.

All the major **combatant countries** used conscription. Britain, however, was unique in two ways: conscripting women and directing labour. At first only unmarried women

GIRL CHOSE HER OWN WORK — FINED

A 23-year-old Sheffield girl gave up her job as a shirt maker, to work in a **munitions** factory.

She was, however, regarded by the Ministry of Labour [a government department] as a 'mobile' worker, and was directed to take employment elsewhere outside the city. She refused, and at Sheffield yesterday she was fined £2.

The girl, Edna Martin, Claywood Road, said she was single when told to work outside Sheffield, but was married last Saturday to a soldier.

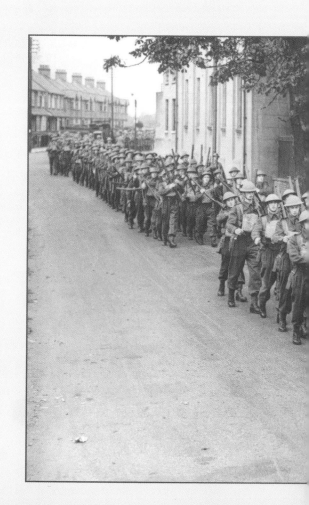

(*Above*) The *News Chronicle* of 7 November 1941 carries this short article reporting the case of a female worker who refused to take up the employment directed by the government.

Evaluation

All national newspapers carried short news items like this. They also had an educational function, letting workers know about government regulations. This article uses no emotive words, that is, words intended to arouse emotion in the reader, and looks reliable, throwing interesting light on the government's direction of labour.

Edna probably swapped shirt-making for munitions work because it was better paid. The government listed unmarried women as 'mobile', meaning they had to work wherever they were sent. Married women were not 'mobile' because it was normal in those days for them to remain at home to look after their husband and children.

Edna was unmarried when she was told to move, which is why she was fined for not going. But the small fine (about one week's wages at that time) suggests the court felt sorry for her. Even so, she may have married just to remain in Sheffield.

The text in square brackets here and in other newspaper articles in this book has been added to explain certain words, terms or references.

Young men of the military reserve, called up in September 1939, get used to army life with a fully-armed route march.

over eighteen and under twenty-one had to register for war work or a woman's branch of the armed services. By 1943 this had been extended to all women between eighteen and fifty.

Directing Labour

Similarly, Britain's was the only government that told all people what work they should do. This applied to men and unmarried women. Many thousands of young women, for example, were moved miles away from their homes to work on farms or in **armament** factories situated in the countryside.

WOMEN'S WAR

Women contributed to Britain's war effort in three vital ways. By 1943 over a quarter of a million had joined one of the three armed services: the Auxiliary Territorial Service (ATS, women's branch of the army), the Women's Auxiliary Air Force (WAAF), and the Women's Royal Naval Service (WRNS – nicknamed 'wrens'). A few service women did very special work indeed. Hand-picked and highly trained, they worked in the intelligence services or operated as spies in enemy-held territory.

Paid and Unpaid

Women undertook a wide variety of other paid work. Hundreds of thousands worked in **munitions** factories, turning out much needed **armaments**. Some 80,000 joined the Women's Land Army, replacing the male farm workers who had been **conscripted**. Because of the shortage of male workers, women took on many tasks that in those days were normally done by men, such as driving buses, welding and brick-laying.

A third group of women, mostly housewives and those over fifty, joined the WVS (Women's Volunteer Service). Their motto was 'Never say no!' The WVS, which had over a quarter of a million members, turned its hand to whatever was needed, from running **air-raid shelters** and collecting **salvage**, to cooking in canteens and helping those who had lost their homes or family in bombing raids.

A HOUSEWIFE'S WORK
by Beveridge

Sir William Beveridge, giving evidence yesterday before the **House of Commons** Committee considering equal war injury **compensation** for men and women, said, 'It seems almost impossible to justify sex differentiation in respect of people not gainfully occupied' [not in paid employment].

But compensation for 'gainfully occupied' people might reasonably be related to their earnings.

Dr Leslie Burgin, MP, asked him whether he regarded a housewife as 'gainfully occupied.'

Sir William: 'I think she is occupied, but not gainfully.'

One Of The Team
Therefore compensation to the housewife should be very little above the minimum subsistence basis [the amount of money needed to live on].

Sir William said he looked upon the housewife as the member of a team. If one member of the team was knocked out, one should inquire how much poorer the team was in consequence. It did not necessarily follow that the women being knocked out impoverished the team as much as if the man were knocked out.

The *Daily Express* of 19 January 1943 reports on the discussion of the issue of war injury compensation.

As straight as any man – many traditionally-minded farmers were surprised to find that members of the Women's Land Army could handle farm machinery just as efficiently as male farm hands had done.

Evaluation

The government paid compensation to adults wounded or injured as a result of the war. This included housewives hurt in air raids. Beveridge was a highly respected Oxford academic whose famous report into the country's social services (1942) laid the foundations of our modern welfare state — the system whereby the government takes care of citizens' basic needs, such as health and welfare.

In this article, however, Beveridge's argument is not very modern. He says that compensation should be paid according to the injured person's earning power. Since women earned less than men (and housewives nothing at all), this clearly meant a raw deal for injured women. Beveridge was probably guided as much by a desire to save the government money at a time of great shortage as by **gender discrimination**. It is also worth noting that during the war Parliament continued to meet and discuss un**censored** the government's actions and policies.

RULES AND REGULATIONS

During the war the government regulated people's lives as never before. The purpose was to put the nation on a war footing and make the best possible use of its resources.

It was feared that enemy air raids would flatten all large towns and cities and cause horrific casualties. To combat the danger, **air-raid shelters** were hastily set up and a strict black-out imposed. This made it illegal for any bright light to be visible outside at night, so it would be far more difficult for enemy bombers to find their targets.

You Must Know These Things

BLACK-OUT RULES FOR ALL HOUSES, CARS

You can be sent to jail or heavily fined, or both, if you do not observe the black-out regulations.

Failure to comply with the regulations involves, on summary conviction [being found guilty by a magistrate's court], liability to imprisonment for a term not exceeding three months, or a fine not exceeding £100, or both.

On conviction on indictment [being found guilty by jury], anyone guilty of an offence against the regulations is liable to imprisonment for a term not exceeding two years, or to a fine not exceeding £500 or both.

The following, states the office of the Lord Privy Seal, are some typical cases of imperfect obscuration [black-out] reported by air raid wardens:-

Shaded lights behind yellow blinds; bars of light showing above dark curtains. Motorists who switch on lights outside their garages while putting their cars away.

Snack bars and similar premises open to the streets which dim the light in the bar itself but allow a bright light to shine out from back rooms, etc.

Front doors of houses and shops opened, allowing light to stream out from the inside.

TO MOTORISTS;-

When the air-raid warning is given, the driver of a motor vehicle must stop and park his vehicle at the side of the road or else in a garage, car park, or open space off the highway ...

No light of any colour whatsoever must be allowed to show from a head-lamp above eye level at a distance of twenty-five feet [7.5 metres] in front of the car.

Feeding the Nation

Importing food and raw materials was expensive and dangerous. Consequently, the government rationed a wide range of goods, from petrol to sugar, and established price controls (fixed limits on how much could be charged for goods) on basic foods, such as eggs and meat. By these means it cut imports, prevented the price of scarce goods soaring and made sure everyone, whatever their income, had enough to eat. Every available corner of land – even public parks and railway embankments – was planted to increase the nation's food supply.

At the onset of war on 4 September 1939, the *Daily Mirror* informs readers of the black-out regulations and the penalties for failing to comply with them.

War on Waste

The manufacture of goods seen as luxuries, like carpets, toys and cameras, was stopped. Factories switched to making war materials, such as uniforms, parachutes and weapons. By the end of the war the regulations were even stricter. For example, lorry drivers were fined for leaving their engines running unnecessarily, and clothing, furniture and household items were made to basic 'utility' standards, that is, they were designed for practical purposes, not to be decorative.

Evaluation

This article is a good example of the government working through the press to get its message across. The *Daily Mirror* is helping the government by passing on information about the black-out. The article's earnest tone and the severe punishments mentioned both reflect the importance attached to the black-out. Getting everyone to participate in something as practical as the black-out was also a way of bringing home the seriousness of the situation to them.

The second part of the article, which lists 'typical cases of imperfect obscuration' suggests that at first the black-out was not taken too seriously. This could easily have been the case since, contrary to expectation, there were almost no bombing raids at that point. The Lord Privy Seal, a minister with roving responsibilities or whose responsibilities were not confined to any one department, was Sir Samuel Hoare.

The suspension dots [...] which appear in the newspaper articles used in this book indicate where portions of the original text have been omitted.

Government warning: Take Care! When the black-out was first started there was a worrying number of accidents, particularly on the roads.

HEALTHY EATING

Food was rationed using coupons. These were issued in ration books. Each book contained coupons for the permitted weekly or monthly amount of a rationed food. These included such everyday items as meat, sugar, butter and eggs. In 1943, for example, a person's margarine ration was four ounces (100 grams) per week. The egg ration was only three per month!

The Black Market

Rationed goods could be bought only by handing over the correct coupon to the shopkeeper at the time of purchase. Each ration book said where the shopping would be done, so the authorities could keep a close eye on what was happening. Even so, it was always possible to buy more than one's ration illegally on the **black market**.

Eating Out

Restaurants and cafes were rationed by limiting the amount of food they received in proportion to the number of customers they served. To help with the war effort, most restaurants offered 'Victory Dishes'. These were made of ingredients that were plentiful, such as carrots. The government set up 'British Restaurants' near people's places of work. They offered a full and wholesome meal for one shilling and twopence (six pence in today's money).

BE SURE OF EGGS
by Alan Thompson

Editor, *Feathered World*

Whether the war is long or short, there will be a great scarcity of eggs for many years to come. If you want them you must produce them yourself.

If you start now, you will find a pullet [a young hen] on the point of lay rather expensive. It costs between 12s. [shillings] and 15s. [between 60 and 75 pence in today's money].

But you can buy younger birds which are not only cheaper but give you some experience before they come into lay.

Don't buy day-old chicks now, if you're a beginner. Choose some fool-proof birds like two- or three-months-old pullets.

A Healthier Nation

Despite the shortages, the health of the nation improved during the war. There were two reasons for this. First, the nation's diet was better because unhealthy foods high in fat and sugar were in short supply. (So, too, were cigarettes.) Second, government regulations ensured that for the first time just about everyone, especially children and the very poor, were properly fed.

A *Daily Herald* article of 16 November 1940 gives some tips on egg production.

Evaluation

Fresh eggs were among the most scarce items of food during the war. This was partly because before the days of factory farming, collecting eggs was labour intensive and most farms were short of hands. In this situation, as the article suggests, many people took to rearing their own chickens for their eggs. Note the technical language that readers were assumed to know — that a 'pullet' is a young hen — and how they were not told what the chickens themselves were to be fed on! The first sentence is interesting, too: the war had already been going on for more than a year, yet Alan Thompson is saying that it might be short. As well as hens, families or groups of families also kept their own pigs and even cows.

Buying rationed soap from the local store, 1942. Ration coupons could be exchanged only at shops previously registered by the shopper.

MAKING DO

Non-food items were also rationed in wartime Britain. Petrol was almost unavailable for civilians. Soap was rationed by weight. Clothes were rationed by item, then by 'points'. In 1942 each adult was permitted clothes worth 48 points. A 'utility' dress (cheaply made of hard-wearing material and not very fashionable) used up 11 points.

Keeping up Appearances

People went to extraordinary lengths to compensate for clothing shortages. Socks and other woollen clothes were darned and re-darned. Old clothes were cut up and made into other garments. (For black-out reasons the government forbade clothes to be made from curtains.) To give the appearance of wearing stockings, white women even painted their legs brown!

PREMIER'S REVIEW OF THE WAR

Increase in output

'ASTOUNDING'

It must also be remembered that all the enemy machines and pilots which are shot down over our island, or over the seas which surround it, are either destroyed or captured, whereas a considerable proportion of our machines and also of our pilots are saved, and many of them soon again come into action.

A vast and admirable system of **salvage**, directed by the Ministry of Aircraft Production, ensures the speediest return to the fighting line of damaged machinery. At the same time the splendid, nay, astounding, increase in the output and repair of British aircraft and engines which Lord Beaverbrook has achieved by a genius for organization and drive which looks like magic – (cheers) – has given us overflowing reserves of every type of aircraft and an ever-mounting stream of production both in quantity and quality. (Cheers.) The enemy is, of course, far more numerous than we are, but our new productions already, as I am advised, largely exceed his, and the American production is only just beginning to flow in. It is a fact that after all this fighting our bomber and fighter strengths are larger than they have ever seen. (Cheers.)

Eating for Victory

Home-made jams and pickles were plentiful. So too were new tinned and dried foods like '**Spam**' – spiced ham – and powdered eggs. The government bombarded the nation with recipes for pies, puddings and soups that made food go further or turned stale left-overs into palatable meals.

(Left) The *Manchester Guardian* of 21 August 1940 reports Prime Minister Winston Churchill's speech in Parliament. In this extract he speaks on the subject of salvage. You can read some more of Churchill's speech on page 26.

Evaluation

They key to understanding this document is the date. Britain was in dire peril. National morale was low. The army had been defeated in France and withdrawn from Dunkirk with the loss of much of its equipment. The Battle of Britain was raging overhead. If the **Nazis** won control of the skies, they would invade Britain.

Prime Minister Churchill's speech, therefore, is not information but **propaganda** aimed to give the impression at home and abroad that Britain could and would win through. This explains the use of grand but unspecific phrases like 'vast and admirable' and 'splendid, nay, astounding'. Lord Beaverbrook was a successful newspaper owner whom Churchill had put in charge of aircraft production because of his business experience and talent for organization.

This is a short extract from the original newspaper article, which reported Prime Minister Churchill's speech in full and with no commentary. It is interesting to note that when this article first appeared, it was quite common for the press to report long speeches in full or at length. Today, we are more used to having them reported in 'soundbites' — short, easy-to-read extracts. The *Manchester Guardian* is now published as the *Guardian*.

Salvage

To make up for the extreme shortage of metals and other materials, the government organized a salvage (recycling) campaign. Thousands of tons of aluminium pots and pans were handed over to the aircraft industry. Miles of iron railings were cut down and used in the manufacture of weapons. Books, carpets, even bones were collected in special bins and put to good use. Interestingly, the feeling of 'pulling together' and 'doing one's bit for the war effort' also helped raise the nation's **morale**.

Although aluminium (needed in aircraft construction) was the most useful salvage, any old iron was welcome – even prams!

15

EVACUATION

During the 1930s the phrase 'the bomber will always get through' was widely used. It meant there was no effective protection against enemy bombs. Actions in the Spanish Civil War (1936-9), such as the devastating bombing of the town of Guernica, seemed to reinforce this view. Furthermore, experts feared poisonous gas bombs would be dropped.

A Million on the Move

As a result, many believed the first few weeks of the war would see massive destruction and loss of life. As a precaution, the government planned a voluntary **evacuation** from target areas of all children and their mothers. The plan was put into action on 1 September 1939, three days before the outbreak of war.

About a million people, mostly children, were moved from the big cities into the countryside. They travelled by train, bus and even boat. Some went with their schools, others with their mothers, and some with just their brothers or sisters. Each child had a label tied to them with their name on it. They took a change of clothes, a packed meal and their gas mask.

Minister Pleased with Progress

WEEK-END PLANS

A good start was made yesterday with the evacuation of children from London, Manchester and other big centres in England, which is to continue over the week-end. The arrangements worked with the greatest smoothness yesterday and last night the Minister of Health, Mr Walter Elliot, expressed his appreciation of the great progress made.

'The railways, the road transport organizations, the local authorities and teachers, and the voluntary workers in reception areas are all playing their part splendidly,' he said.

The time that evacuation will take to be complete will vary in different areas. The removal of the school children will continue in the areas where it is not already completed, and this will be followed by the evacuation of young children, accompanied by their mothers or by some other responsible person, the expectant mothers, the blind and any cripples [people with disabilities] who have received instructions that they will be moved.

Strange Experiences

Evacuation was a strange experience for both the children and the volunteers who housed them. Many children from the poorest families had never seen the countryside before. They were shocked by the sights and sounds – and their new families were equally shocked by some of the children's poverty and dirtiness.

The *Manchester Guardian* of 2 September 1939 reports on the beginning of the evacuation programme.

Government regulations said that each evacuee child was to pack underwear, spare shoes, socks or stockings, a coat, a sweater, handkerchiefs and night clothes. Children from poor families (not those in this picture) had never owned many of these items.

As the expected bombing did not happen, by Christmas 1939 many evacuees had returned home. A second evacuation followed in the summer of 1940, when the really heavy bombing started. Finally, in reaction to **V1** and **V2** missile attacks on London, there was a third evacuation in 1944.

Evaluation

With the country on the verge of war, it was highly unlikely that a minister would criticize a major government operation. Moreover, evacuation was voluntary because the government did not believe it would be possible or right to force people out of their homes. Therefore, Walter Elliot was keen to report on the evacuation programme as favourably as possible. This was to encourage more families to take it up. For these reasons the article is not reliable evidence about the success or even the popularity of evacuation. We are given no numbers, for example, and not even a few words from a mother or child being evacuated.

DAD'S ARMY

After the **evacuation** of the British Army from Dunkirk in May and June 1940, Hitler hoped to invade Britain (Operation Sealion, planned for 17 September). British beaches were hastily defended with concrete anti-tank devices and pill boxes – small concrete or brick forts with narrow openings for guns. Inland, more pill boxes were constructed and defensive lines drawn across the countryside.

To help man the defences, in May 1940 War Secretary Anthony Eden proposed a force of Local Defence Volunteers (LDV). Thousands of men came forward and within a year the LDV (re-named the Home Guard and nicknamed 'Dad's Army') numbered about half a million men.

Volunteers with Pitch Forks

The efficiency of the Home Guard varied enormously. Some units, like that shown in the famous BBC TV comedy series *Dad's Army*, were hopelessly inefficient. Others, organized and led by veterans of World War I, were altogether more professional.

LDV DELAY EXPLAINED

Call Likely at Any Time

Mr Churchill's announce- ment yesterday that more than 500,000 men are now enrolled in the Local Defence Volunteers will have surprised many thousands who registered at police stations a month ago and have heard nothing further.

The explanation, given by an official of the War Office, is that in the majority of cases this apparent neglect is due to the authorized complement [required number] having been completed. The author- ities do not want to lose men who have registered but have not been called upon for service, because it may be necessary at any moment to extend the complement and then those men would be wanted at once.

A *Daily Telegraph* article of 19 June 1940 reports on a problem with recruitment to the Home Guard.

Evaluation

The interesting point about this article is what it does not say. It was written after the Dunkirk evacuation, when the country was likely to be invaded. The *Telegraph* knew that in this situation criticism of the government would be seriously unpatriotic and might well be **censored**.

Nevertheless, it looks as if recruitment to the Home Guard (LDV) had run into problems and the paper felt it had a duty to report this. The first paragraph hints at an administrative failure. Clearly, many more volunteers had come forward than the administration could cope with. The paper does not give its own reason for this but merely cites the government's: the 'authorized complement' (required number) was 'completed'. Is this convincing?

Volunteers were aged between sixteen and sixty-five. They were either too old or too young to be recruited into the regular forces or they worked in 'reserve occupations' (see page 6). Armed with any weapons they could get their hands on – at first, even farm implements, later replaced by US and Canadian rifles – the Home Guard were not disbanded until 1944. In its later years it swapped anti-invasion duties for air-raid protection work.

Is this how you do it, corporal? Members of the Home Guard at rifle training. Had Britain been invaded in 1940, it is thought that professional troops would have swiftly brushed aside the amateur Home Guard.

BLITZ

The German tactic of 'blitzkrieg' ('lightning war') meant swift attacks with aircraft, artillery and armour along a narrow **front**. The British adopted the word for the bombing attacks on British cities, 1940-41: the **Blitz**.

By May 1941 the medium bombers of the **Luftwaffe** (the German Air Force) had dropped 54,420 tonnes of bombs, killing 40,000 people, injuring 86,000 and destroying 2 million homes. Its own losses were very high, especially in August and September 1940 when their raids were mostly in daylight. By November the Luftwaffe had lost more than 1,100 planes and 2,500 crew.

(Left) **The Manchester Guardian of 9 September 1940 reports on a weekend bombing of London.**

99 NAZIS DOWN IN SATURDAY'S INDISCRIMINATE RAIDS

Goering in personal charge of campaign

Some 400 people were killed and 1,300 to 1,400 seriously injured in mass air raids on the London area which began in daylight on Saturday and were continued throughout the night. The first attack was directed against the docks, where fires were started which guided the later raiders. In the second attack, after dark, the bombing became indiscriminate, and working-class houses in the East End suffered the most.

Last night there was another bombing attack spread over a wide area of London, but this time there were no big concentrations of planes and the casualties were comparatively few …

Saturday's attacks cost the Germans 99 'planes, of which 21 fell to AA [anti-aircraft] fire. Twenty-two British fighters were lost, but nine pilots are safe. These final figures were announced last night.

It should be recognized that while the damage done in Saturday's raids may be judged from the local viewpoint as fairly severe it must not be regarded as serious when looked at against the general background of the war, the more so since we had been prepared for far more severe damage ever since the war broke out.

The Will to Resist

The Blitz was intended to break British **morale**. It had the opposite effect, toughening the will to resist. As fighter planes, **barrage balloons**, searchlights and **anti-aircraft guns** tackled the enemy overhead, civilians, alerted by air-raid sirens, took refuge in **air-raid shelters**.

The Blitz created a massive force of air-raid wardens, firemen, **fire spotters**, **runners**, first-aiders, emergency workers and canteen staff. Many of those who worked in these services were unpaid volunteers.

Evaluation

This article is fascinating example of the way newspapers presented news (as they still do) to give it a particular emphasis. The headline, for example, tells of the number of enemy planes downed, not the damage or British losses.

The third paragraph emphasizes the nine pilots who were saved, not the thirteen who died. Finally, the last paragraph tries to reassure readers that the damage was less than it seemed. The article also criticizes the bombing for being 'indiscriminate' and for destroying the homes of innocent civilians.

Note how the enemy are called **'Nazis'**, not Germans, and the way an individual, Goering, is blamed. Hermann Goering was commander-in-chief of the German Air Force.

The centre of Liverpool after the city was blitzed, on 29 November 1940. By 1942 some 7,500 Liverpudlians had been killed or wounded by enemy bombing.

TAKING SHELTER

A wide range of **air-raid shelters** was used during World War II. The simplest was the Morrison Shelter, a type of cage of steel and wire that was placed in the most secure part of a building. It was named after Secretary of State for Home Affairs, Herbert Morrison.

More comfortable was the Anderson Shelter, named after Home Secretary Sir John Anderson. It consisted of an arch of steel sheets, most effective when at least partially buried in the ground. Many families used neither a Morrison nor an Anderson Shelter but took refuge in their cellar or under the stairs.

Cave dwellers

Some of the bigger cities built large, purpose-built air-raid shelters. Fitted with lighting and toilets, and made of reinforced concrete, they gave protection to upwards of 100 people. Nevertheless, even the strongest shelters offered no protection against a direct hit from a high-explosive bomb.

The only really safe places were the deeper London Underground stations (the safest were on the Northern Line) and natural caves, such as those at Chislehurst in Kent and beneath Liverpool and Nottingham. The Chislehurst caves were so popular that special trains linked them to the capital.

From an ARP correspondent

Tube 'night life' is beginning to assume a regular form. It is in many ways much different from that of the night life of ordinary London public shelters. Surroundings, though familiar in some ways, are strange in others. There is no noise of bombs and barrage [anti-aircraft fire], but there is the traffic of train and passenger.

Queues for admittance form early, but the London Transport Board is lenient and they wind into the bowels of the earth about 3.30. Down below a blanket or a bag is sometimes left to mark a berth while the owner emerges for a spell on other business than keeping a place. Nor is the claim often jumped.

The shelterers below are ruled by the stationmaster … and by his foreman porter, assisted where necessary by the police (women as well as men). In addition there are shelter wardens from the various local authorities to help. The atmosphere is generally a friendly one …

Music is allowed and welcomed, provided the musicians stop when the vast majority want to go to sleep, which is about ten, and provided there is no attempt to take a collection. There is singing, with an occasional chorus for 'the ladies only' which takes the place of a comic turn, judging by the subsequent laughter. Favourite tunes vary from station to station.

This *Manchester Guardian* article of 19 November 1940 describes sheltering from air-raid attacks in the London Underground.

ARP wardens talk to Londoners sheltering in the Bounds Green underground station, December 1940. Providing adequate toilet facilities was one of the officials' major headaches.

Evaluation

Is the correspondent picking out only the best features of sheltering in the London Underground? He does not mention the smell of unwashed bodies crowded together, for example, nor the inadequate toilet facilities, nor the children crying in the night.

On the other hand, it is possible that the article is genuine in its up-beat mood. Many people had fond memories of the war. They remembered how shared hardships had brought the best out of people, building a strong community spirit and willingness of co-operate. Something of that mood — especially the community singing — is reflected in this extract. 'ARP' stood for Air Raid Precautions.

KEEP SMILING

Most professional sport – cricket and football in particular – was cancelled for the duration of the war because the players were in the forces. Nevertheless, horse racing continued and there was plenty of amateur sport to entertain players and watchers. As well as providing news, the BBC also broadcast music and comedy programmes. The most famous was *ITMA* (*It's That Man Again*), starring the comedian Tommy Handley.

ENSA

The government realized that keeping up **morale** was as important as more obvious war work, such as resisting invasion. To this end it established the Entertainments National Service Association (ENSA). This was a government-funded organization whose purpose was to make people feel positive and cheerful, despite being surrounded by the difficulties and horrors of war.

(Left) These film reviews appeared in the *Daily Telegraph* of 15 July 1940.

FILM NOTES

FORMBY FARCE

Let George Do It

(*Empire*)

Gone With The Wind has gone at last. In its place is a farce starring the most popular British film actor of the day, George Formby. He is mistaken for a British agent, helps to unmask a gang giving tips to U-boats [German submarines], is projected through high windows and a torpedo tube, is threatened with sudden death and slow roast-ing in a loaf of bread. Though Mr Formby's dental grin and assumption of oafish cunning do not convulse me as they do others, I found *Let George Do It* good fun, and Formby fans will be enchanted.

In the same programme is a stirring little short, *Britain At Bay*, sponsored by the Ministry of Information, with a commentary by JB Priestly.

About eighty percent of the nation's entertainers joined ENSA. No one, however famous, earned more than £10 a week, which helped keep the total bill for ENSA throughout the war down to £14 million. It provided all kinds of entertainment, from bands to stand-up comedians, wherever they were needed. Most performances were in halls, theatres and factory canteens. Several performers went abroad to entertain troops in the field.

Evaluation

This somewhat stuffy film review illustrates how the entertainment industry played its part in the fight for victory. *Gone With The Wind* was an American film that had nothing to do with the war. Its replacement, *Let George Do It*, was possibly not a very good movie but a form of mild **propaganda**. Its plot — a British comedian helping to defeat the enemy — was both amusing (to some) and patriotic in the way it showed how the enemy could be outwitted, even by a **media** clown. By 1940 there was no escaping the war, not even in the cinema.

Because it was made by the Ministry of Information, the second film was more obviously propaganda. Its title, *Britain At Bay*, suggests a fierce animal (perhaps the British bulldog) forced into a corner where it refuses to surrender. The date of this review together with the film title suggests the picture had been made in a hurry since the Dunkirk **evacuation** of May and June 1940.

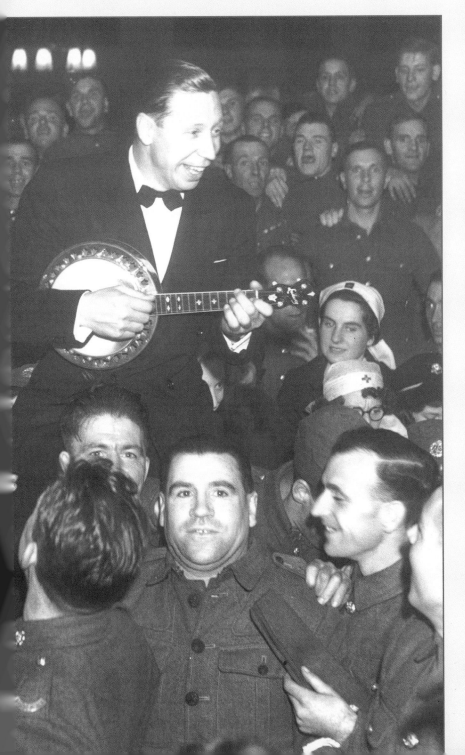

George Formby, the Northern comedian and musician, plays before an audience of some 2,000 troops, 1939. The double-meaning lyrics of his songs were a great hit with the soldiers.

THE WAR OF WORDS

More than any previous war, World War II was fought with words as well as weapons. There were three main reasons for this.

First, in 1939, when the war broke out, two major powers – the USA and the USSR – were neutral. As these two countries were potential **allies**, both Britain and Germany slanted information to create a good impression with them. Second, the use of the radio (or 'wireless' as it was then called) meant that information could be beamed right into the homes of the enemy. Finally, victory depended heavily on the **morale** of the mass of civilians not in arms, and this was influenced by the information they received.

Premier's review of the War
THE DEBT TO OUR AIRMEN

The gratitude of every home in our island, in our Empire, and indeed throughout the world except in the abodes of the guilty goes out to the British airmen who, undaunted by odds, unweakened by their constant challenge and mortal danger, are turning the tide of world war by their prowess and their devotion.

Never in the field of human conflict was so much owed by so many to so few. (Prolonged cheers.) All hearts go out to the fighter pilots, whose brilliant actions we see with our own eyes day after day but we must never forget that all the time, night after night, month after month, our bomber squadrons travel far into Germany, find their targets in the darkness by the highest navigational skill, aim their attacks, often under the heaviest fire, often at serious loss, with deliberate, careful precision, and inflict shattering blows upon the whole of the technical and war-making structure of the Nazi power. (Cheers.)

On no part of the Royal Air Force does the weight of the war fall more heavily than on the daylight bombers, who will play an invaluable part in the case of an invasion and whose unflinching zeal it has been necessary in the meantime on numerous occasions to restrain.

Boosting Morale

Propaganda – information intended to persuade or deceive – took many forms. On the radio these ran from Churchill's speeches to the broadcasts from Germany of the pro-**Nazi** William Joyce, who was mocked as 'Lord Haw-Haw' because of his exaggerated upper-class accent. Other propaganda included films (see page 24), posters, books and newspaper articles. The British generally responded better to humour than earnestness.

Prime Minister Winston Churchill's speech to the **House of Commons** is reported in the *Manchester Guardian* of 21 August 1940.

Although Churchill is famous for his dogged talk about never surrendering, this 1940 poster tries to look beyond resistance to future offensives.

Evaluation

As so often in his speeches at this time, Churchill gives his audience no specific information. Instead, he offers pure rhetoric — a stirring and persuasive way of speaking — intended to raise the morale of the British people, lower that of the enemy and tell the world that Britain was winning the war.

Note how Churchill uses exaggeration (hyperbole), 'every home ... throughout the world'; how he blackens the enemy, by calling them 'the guilty' and 'the Nazi power'; and how he repeats himself for effect, 'night after night, month after month' or, most famously of all, 'Never in the field of human conflict was so much owed by so many to so few.'

Churchill is deliberately creating a 'David v Goliath' image of the war. This was to appeal to neutral America as he knew Britain could not win unless the USA joined the war on its side.

FRIENDS AND FOES

In the early years of the war Britain was home to thousands of **allies** – French, Dutch, Norwegians, Poles and others – who had fled there to continue their fight against the **Nazis**. Polish pilots, for instance, played an important role in the Battle of Britain. Many Canadians, Australians and New Zealanders were based in Britain, too. There was also a small number of enemy prisoners of war.

The GI Invasion

The USA entered the war in December 1941 and from 1942 onwards thousands of Americans began arriving in Britain. Just before the D-Day landings in France (June 1944) Britain was host to about 1.5 million foreign military personnel. American GIs (from 'Government Issue' stamped on their clothes) were generally the most popular. They were optimistic, had money in their pockets (a US soldier earned almost five times as much as British one) and had access to luxuries, such as nylon stockings, that had been virtually unavailable in Britain for years.

Not surprisingly, many love affairs developed between British women and foreign servicemen. A number ended in marriage and the emigration of British wives after the war. Some 18,000 went to live in Canada and over 80,000 of them ('GI brides') to the USA.

Their Homes Will Be Made in Strange Lands

This is advice to young wives, the girls who fell in love with Poles, French sailors, Dutchmen, Norwegians, Americans and Canadians.

You're beginning to wonder what your married life will be like in your husband's country.

You want to know how soon after the war, if not before, you will be able to go to that new land and begin to set up house.

* * *

Mrs A McK of Newcastle, married a Canadian.

He is the son of a private farmer and he will live with his father when he gets out of the Air Force. Mrs McK writes:–

'Donald says he wants me to get ready to go to Canada very soon. His mother had three sons, no daughters and she is anxious to have me out there.

'Do you think I can go to Canada soon and get to know my husband's people before we have to settle down as a family?

'I think it would be wiser for me to go on ahead and break the ice.'

You've no trouble in front of you, Mrs McK. The Canadian Government is welcoming new wives with great generosity.

This advice to war brides appeared in the *Daily Mirror* of 22 September 1944.

Evaluation

This is an extract from the *Daily Mirror's* **agony aunt** page, known as 'Mary Ferguson's Home Service'. The opening is an interesting reminder that British women struck up relationships with service personnel of many nations, not just glamorous 'Yanks'. As a result, the war played an important part in breaking down international barriers.

The traditional view of the male as the head of the household is also reflected. It is assumed that women like Mrs McK are leaving Britain to go to their new husbands' countries rather than their husbands staying in Britain.

Given the article's date, it is perhaps surprising to find the end of the war being talked about and planned for. In fact, the war did not end in Europe for another eight months and in the Far East for almost a year.

Australian soldiers with English girlfriends, 1939-40. Soldiers and airmen from various corners of the British Empire and Commonwealth played a vital role in the British armed forces throughout the war.

TIMELINE

1936:
Britain's first air-raid shelters built.

1938:
ATS formed.
WAAF formed.
WVS formed.

1939:
WRNS formed.
Women's Land Army formed.
September — Evacuation of mothers and children from large cities and towns.
War begins (3rd). Blackout starts. First air raids. Petrol rationed.
ENSA formed.

1940:
January — Food rationing begins.
June — Second evacuation.
July-Sept — Battle of Britain.
September — London Blitz begins (to May 1941).
November — Coventry Blitz.

1941:
March — Women conscripted.
Clydebank Blitz.
May — Liverpool Blitz.
June — Clothes rationing starts.
December — USA joins the war.

1942:
May-June — Canterbury Blitz.
July — Austerity regulations limit amount of materials used in many branches of manufacturing.

1943:
Many evacuees returning home.
May — Allies winning Battle of the Atlantic.
June — Children's clothes rationing begins.
July — Women up to the age of 51 registered for employment.

1944:
July — London hit by V1 missiles. Third evacuation.

1945:
May — War ends in Europe. Evacuees start returning home.

1954:
All rationing finally ends.

GLOSSARY

ACT: Law passed by parliament.

AGONY AUNT: Someone who gives advice in a newspaper or magazine to readers who write asking for help with their personal problems.

AIR-RAID SHELTER: Shelter, often underground that was more or less proof against bomb blast.

ALLIES: Britain, USA, France, USSR and other countries that fought together in World War II.

ANTI-AIRCRAFT GUN: Gun for shooting at aircraft.

ARMAMENTS: Weapons and ammunition of every kind.

ARMED FORCES: Army, navy and air force.

BARRAGE BALLOON: Gas-filled balloon trailing cables to deter enemy bombers. Bombers had to fly high enough to miss the balloons, making it more difficult for them to aim their bombs.

BLACK MARKET: Illegal buying and selling of goods and food.

BLITZ: Intensive bombing of a city, from German word *blitzkrieg* or 'lightning war'.

CENSOR/CENSORSHIP: To prevent the publication or display of material that it is thought undesirable or unsuitable to make public.

COMBATANT COUNTRIES: Countries actively involved in fighting a war.

COMPENSATION: Money paid to make up for an injury or other hurt.

CONSCRIPT/CONSCRIPTION: To make people join the armed forces or do other war work.

EVACUATE/EVACUATION: To move to a safe place.

FRONT: Place where opposing forces come into contact with each other.

GENDER DISCRIMINATION: To treat people differently according to whether they are male or female.

HOUSE OF COMMONS: The elected 'lower house' in Parliament.

IMPORT: Bring something in from another country.

LUFTWAFFE: German Air Force.

MEDIA: General word for newspapers, TV, films, radio and other forms of mass communication.

MORALE: Mood or spirit of a group of people usually working together.

MUNITIONS: Weapons and ammunition.

NAZI: Germany's National Socialist Party, led by Adolf Hitler.

PROPAGANDA: Slanted information intended to affect morale.

RUNNERS: People who carried the news of fires to the fire brigade, requesting help. Sometimes they also carried requests for other emergency services.

SALVAGE: Material for recycling.

SPAM: Spiced ham, usually tinned.

SPOTTERS: People who kept watch from high places for incendiary bombs and the sudden fires they started.

TOTAL WAR: War involving all civilian and military resources.

V1 & V2: Jet-propelled missiles fired at London. The V1 was a pilotless plane with short wings. The supersonic V2 was the first modern long-range, rocket-propelled missile.

RESOURCES

Books

Caroline Lang, *Keep Smiling Through: Women in the Second World War*, CUP, 1989.

Stewart Ross, *At Home in World War Two: Women's War*, Evans, 2002.

Stewart Ross, *At Home in World War Two: Rationing*, Evans, 2002.

Stewart Ross, *At Home in World War Two: Evacuation*, Evans, 2002.

Stewart Ross, *At Home in World War Two: Blitz*, Evans, 2002.

Terry Deary, *Horrible Histories: The Blitzed Brits*, Hippo, 1994.

Robert Westall, *Children of the Blitz*, Macmillan, 1995.

Brian Barton, *The Blitz*, Blackstaff, 1999.

Websites

bbc.co.uk/history/wwtwo.shtml

iwm.org.uk/lambeth/lambeth.htm

angelfire.com/la/raeder/England.html

atschool.eduweb.co.uk/nettsch/time/wlife.html

pnc.com.au/~insight/blitz-1.html

maksites.com/PART1.htm

british-forces.com/world_war2

historyplace.com/worldwar2

maelstrom.stjohns.edu/archives/memories.html

Visit www.learn.co.uk, the award-winning educational website backed by the *Guardian*, for exciting historical resources and online events.

Places to visit

Aerospace Museum, Cosford, Shropshire

Battle of Britain Museum, Hawkinge, Kent

Cabinet War Rooms, London

Chartwell, Kent, home of Winston Churchill

Coventry Cathedral

German Military Underground Hospital, Guernsey

German Occupation Museum, Guernsey

'Hellfire Corner', Dover Castle

Imperial War Museum, London.

Imperial War Museum North, Manchester

Island Fortress Occupation Museum, Jersey

London Experience, Trocadero Centre

Museum of London

RAF Museum, Hendon

White Cliffs Experience, Dover

Most local museums also have excellent information and displays on their town or region during World War II.

INDEX